GEOGRAPHYWISE

COASTS

Jen Green

Published by Wayland in 2012

Wayland
Hachette Children's Books
338 Euston Road
London NW1 3BH

Wayland Australia
Level 17/207 Kent Street
Sydney, NSW 2000

Editorial director: Rasha Elsaeed
Designer: Tim Mayer, MayerMedia
Illustrator: Peter Bull Art Studio
Consultant: Meg Gillett

British Library Cataloguing in Publication Data

Green, Jen.
Geographywise.
Coasts.
1. Coasts--Juvenile literature.
I. Title
910'.02146-dc22

ISBN 9780750269438

First published in 2010 by Wayland

This paperback edition published by Wayland in 2012

Printed in China

Wayland is a division of Hachette Children's Books,
an Hachette UK company.
www.hachette.co.uk

Picture acknowledgements
Front Cover © ISTOCK, Back Cover © Xi Zhi Nong/naturepl.com, Page 4 © ISTOCK, Page 5(t) © ISTOCK, Page 5(b) © Wayland, Page 6 © N-188-0169 Craig Tuttle/Corbis, Page 7(t) © Wayland, Page 7(b) © 492-3309, Rob Cousins/Robert Harding, Page 8(t) © Wayland, Page 8b © 1240183,Billy Black/Bluegreenpictures.com, Page 9© AAFB001444 Jason Hawkes/Corbis, Page10 © 42-15498589 ParksVictoria/Handout/Reuters/Corbis, Page 10(l) © a0078-000161 John W Banagan/Getty Images, Page 11(t) © Wayland, Page 11(b) © ISTOCK, Page 12 © 51913110 Ross Hoddinott/Bluegreenpictures.com, Page 13 © BT001098 Corbis, Page 14 (t) © Wayland, Page 14(l) © 89615098 Stocktrek Images/Getty Images, Page 15 © ISTOCK, Page 16 © ISTOCK, Page 17 © Wayland, Page 18 © 01094630 Brandon Cole/naturepl.com, Page 19 © ISTOCK, Page 20 © IH122301 Joel W. Rogers/Corbis, Page 21 © Pic 35 Biosphoto/Coupard Michel/Still Pictures, Page22/23 © ISTOCK,Page 23(tr) © 277126-001 Ian Murphy/Getty Images, Page 24((t) © Wayland, Page 24(b) © ISTOCK, Page 25 © 51913110 Getty Images, Page 26 © 82133425 Jeff Hunter/Getty Images, Page 27 © 4906-E1E1 Ian Harwood/Ecoscene, Page 28 © Wayland, Page 29 © 01090557 Brandon Cole/naturepl.com,

Contents

What are coasts?

The coast is the place where the dry land meets the sea. The scenery on coasts is amazingly varied. There may be towering **cliffs**, sandy beaches or rocky **headlands**. Where rivers meet the coast you may find **mudflats** or a swampy **delta**.

Coasts provide homes for all sorts of wildlife. Rocky shores, beaches and mudflats all have different plants and animals. For thousands of years, people have also lived on coasts.

Rocky headlands and all kinds of dramatic scenery can be seen on coasts. These jagged rocks are found in Devon, UK.

UNBELIEVABLE!

Canada is the country with the longest coastline, stretching around 245,000 kilometres. Russia has the second-longest coast at 103,000 kilometres long.

The shape of the coast is always changing. Cliffs and headlands crumble or the sea dumps sand and pebbles. People also change the shape of coasts, for example by building a sea wall or a **marina**. This book will explain about how **coastal** landscapes form, and how people, plants and animals live on coasts.

Many people go to the coast for their holidays. This beach is near the city of Rio de Janeiro, Brazil.

This map shows the shape of the world's coastlines. All of Earth's large landmasses are surrounded by seas and oceans. Coasts form the border between land and sea.

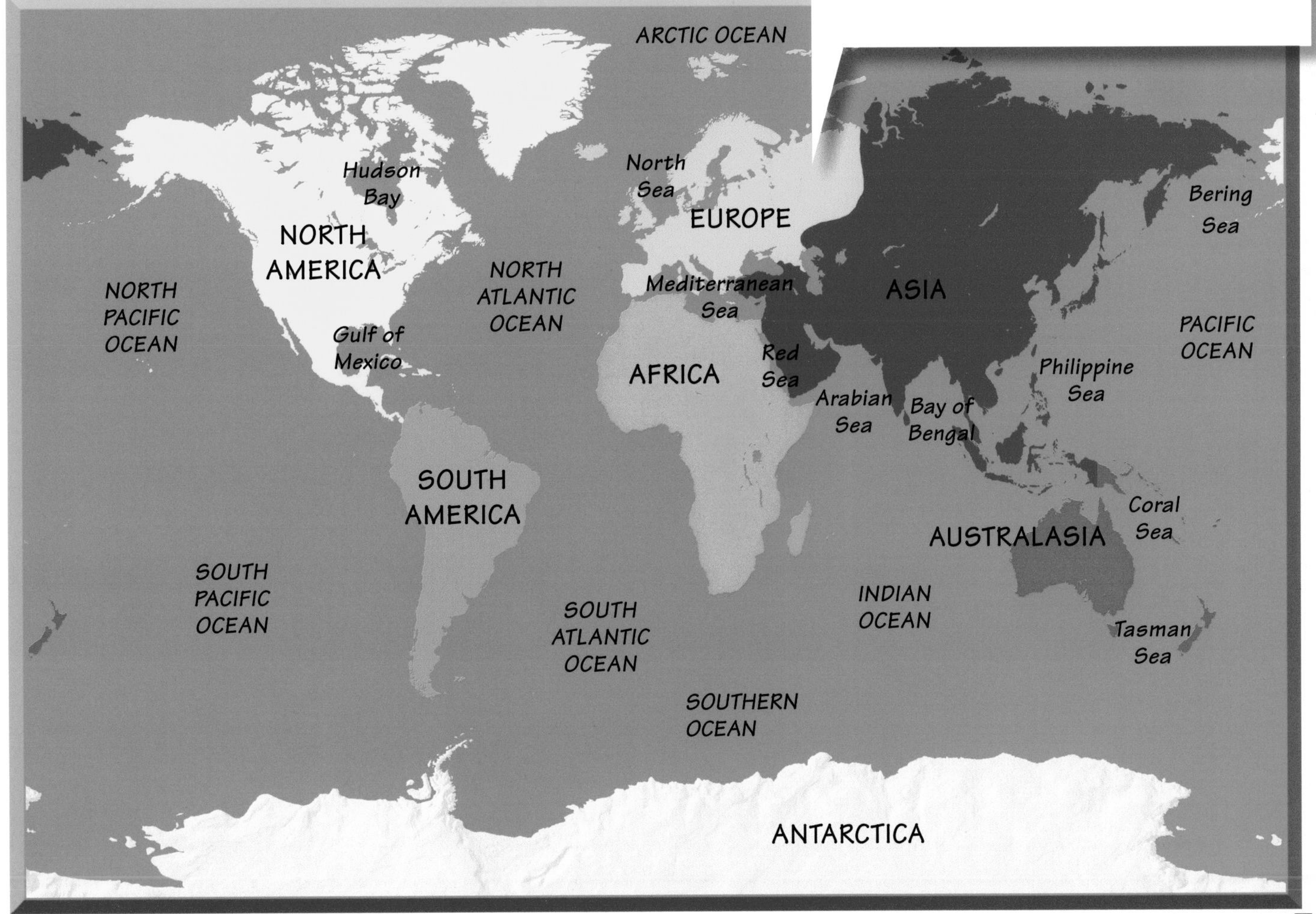

Shaping the shore

The landscape at the coast is mainly shaped by the sea. Waves beat at the shore every minute of every day. Water, pebbles and sand are swept against the rocks. Cracks in rocks get wider, and eventually bits break off. Coastal rocks gradually **erode** (wear away).

Waves are caused by winds blowing across the sea's surface. Waves rise high in shallow water, and then crash onto the shore.

Twice a day, the sea surges up the shore and then falls back again. These changes are called **tides**. They are mainly caused by the tug of the Moon's **gravity** on the Earth. As the Moon circles our planet it pulls the sea towards it. This produces a mound of water, which sweeps across the oceans. When it reaches the coast, it forms a high tide.

UNBELIEVABLE!

The Bay of Fundy in eastern Canada has the world's biggest tides. The sea rises and falls by up to 16 metres here. The Severn Estuary in western Britain also has extreme tides.

Where waves strike the coast at an angle, they shift sand and pebbles sideways. This process is called **longshore drift**. The diagram below shows how it works.

Longshore drift happens where waves hit the shore at an angle. The arrows show how sand and pebbles move in a zigzag.

Bays and headlands

Some parts of the coast erode more quickly than others. It depends on the strength of waves and tides, and also on the rocks found at the coast. Soft rocks, such as chalk, erode more quickly than hard rocks, such as granite.

Where waves eat into soft rocks, a deep **bay** or shell-shaped **cove** develops. Hard rocks last much longer, forming headlands jutting out to sea.

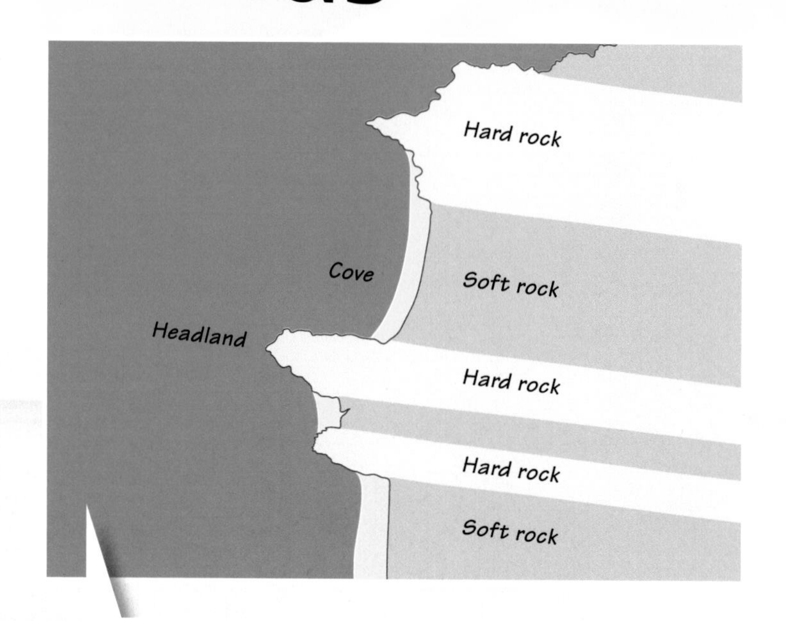

Coastal erosion forms bays or coves in areas of soft rock. Bands of hard rock are left sticking out to sea as headlands.

Waves and currents transport sand and pebbles along the coast. Strong currents and powerful waves have enough energy to shift rocky debris. Where currents and waves become weak in sheltered bays and coves, they drop their rocky fragments. Sand and pebbles then wash ashore to form a beach.

At this bay, Lulworth Cove, in Dorset, southern Britain, the sea has eroded soft rocks to make an almost circular cove.

SHIPWRECKED!

Over the centuries, many ships have been wrecked on rocky headlands. In days gone by, people called wreckers lured ships onto rocks using lights. Sailors confused by the lights steered onto the rocks, then the wreckers got the booty!

Cliffs, arches and caves

No two coastlines are exactly alike. Cliffs form where hills, made of hard rocks, meet the sea. As waves crash against the base of the cliff, they cut a deep notch. Eventually the rock on top collapses, and the cliff moves a little further inland.

*A group of sea **stacks** called the Twelve Apostles (left and above) lies off the coast of southeastern Australia. In 2005, a 50-metre stack collapsed into the sea.*

Some coasts are being eroded by more than a metre each year. The soft rocks of Holderness in northeast Britain are crumbling by about two metres each year!

Where waves beat against both sides of a rocky headland, twin caves may form. Eventually these caves meet and form an arch. As erosion continues, the top of the arch collapses. This leaves a pillar called a stack standing in the sea.

The diagram below shows how the sea can erode caves and later an arch in a headland. Durdle Door in southern Britain, shown in the photo below, is an example of an arch. Later still, the arch roof crumbles to leave a stack.

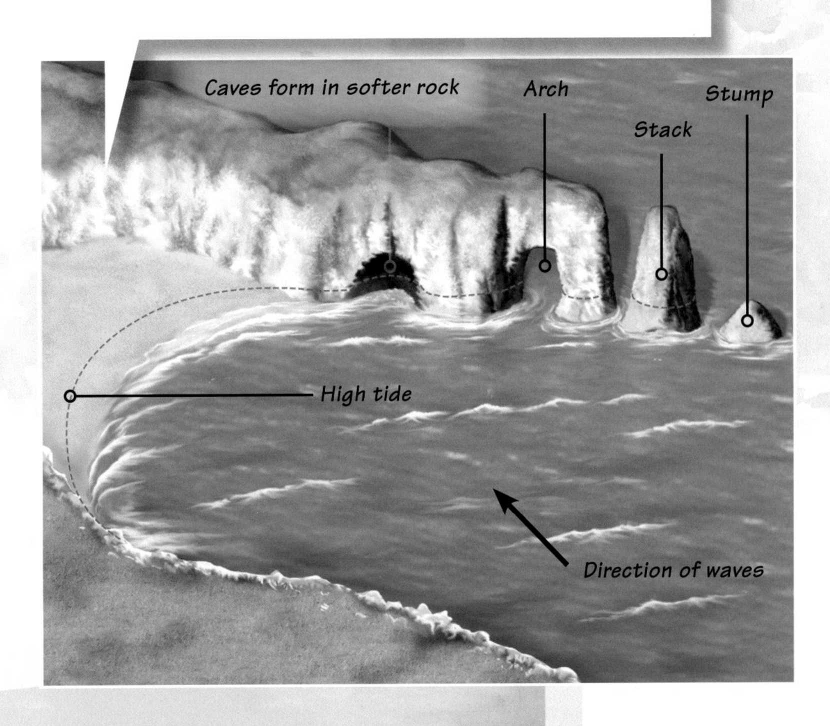

LAND BELOW SEA LEVEL

People try to slow down erosion by building walls on the coast. In Holland, sea walls called dykes run for hundreds of kilometres. Much of the land behind the dykes is below sea level, so they are vital to keep the sea from flooding the land!

Beaches, dunes and deltas

Beaches are made of rocky **debris** that has eroded from cliffs or been carried out to sea by rivers. The beach may be made of sand or pebbles. Sand is made of tiny bits of rock or shell that have been smashed by the waves. Pebbles are small chunks of rock worn smooth by the waves.

Sand **dunes** form where the wind piles heaps of loose sand behind the beach. High winds and storms can shift the dunes along the beach or even inland.

If grass grows on sand dunes, it can help to anchor the sand in place and stop it blowing inland.

A delta is an area of flat, swampy land at the mouth of a river. Deltas are made of **silt** – mud or sand carried down by the river. Where the river meets the sea, the current slows, and the river drops silt to build up a delta. This is called **deposition**.

This satellite image shows the Ganges Delta on the shores of the Indian Ocean. It is the world's largest delta. The river splits into many channels as it weaves through the silt.

UNBELIEVABLE!

The sand on most beaches is yellow, but it may also be white, black or even pink! Volcanic islands sometimes have black beaches, made of smashed volcanic rock. Sand made of bits of shell is usually white, but in a few places the shells are mostly red, which makes the sand pink!

Islands and coral reefs

Islands are areas of land surrounded by the sea. They often have very long coastlines! Islands far out in the ocean are usually the tops of underwater volcanoes. When a volcano **erupts** on the seabed, **lava** piles up to make an undersea mountain. Eventually the mountain becomes so tall it pokes out of the sea to form an island.

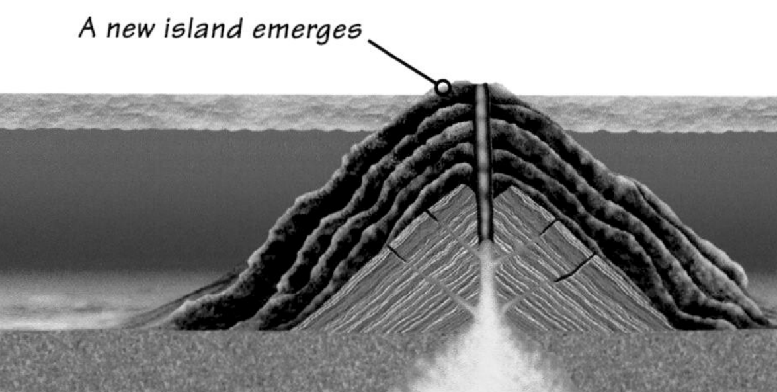

This diagram shows how lava from an undersea volcano slowly builds up and erupts to form an island.

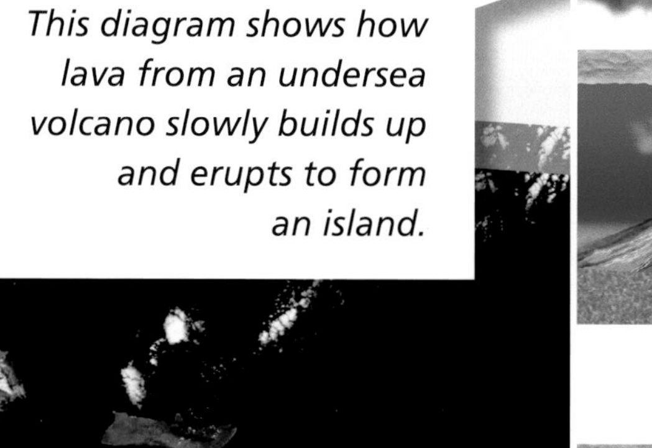

The Hawaiian islands in the Pacific Ocean are the tops of a chain of undersea volcanoes. Some of the volcanoes rise 10,000 metres from the seabed – much higher than Mount Everest.

The Great Barrier Reef off eastern Australia stretches for over 2,000 kilometres. It is the world's largest coral reef.

Some islands, such as Britain, lie close to the mainland. Britain was joined to the rest of Europe thousands of years ago, when sea levels were lower. Then the sea rose. Water flooded what is now the English Channel, and Britain became an island.

Coral reefs lie off many tropical coasts and islands. They are actually large piles of small, chalky skeletons – the remains of sea creatures that look like anemones. When the coral creatures die, their skeletons build up on top of each other to form the reef.

HOT SPRINGS

Iceland is a large volcanic island in the North Atlantic Ocean. Volcanoes heat underground springs that bubble up to the surface. People bathe in warm pools fed by these hot springs.

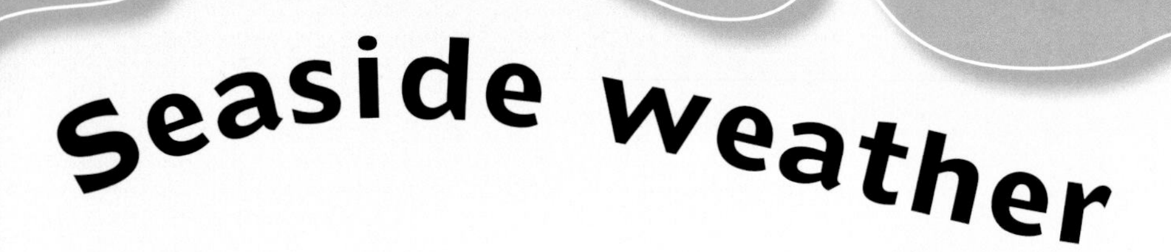

Seaside weather

Coasts have very different weather to places that lie far inland. The weather is often wet, because winds blowing off the ocean bring clouds and rain. Coasts are breezy, too, with winds blowing day and night.

Coasts are usually wetter and windier than inland areas. These palm trees are tossing in a violent storm.

UNBELIEVABLE!

Storms produce rough seas that can wreck islands and coastal towns. In 1900, a violent storm hit the port of Galveston in southern USA. Waves swept all over the town, which stood on a small island. About 6,000 people drowned.

The weather is generally mild near the coast. This is because the sea warms up more slowly than the land, which makes the coast cool in summer. The sea also keeps its heat for longer, which keeps the coast warm in winter. Conditions are not always calm, however. Storms can bring howling winds, lashing rain and towering waves.

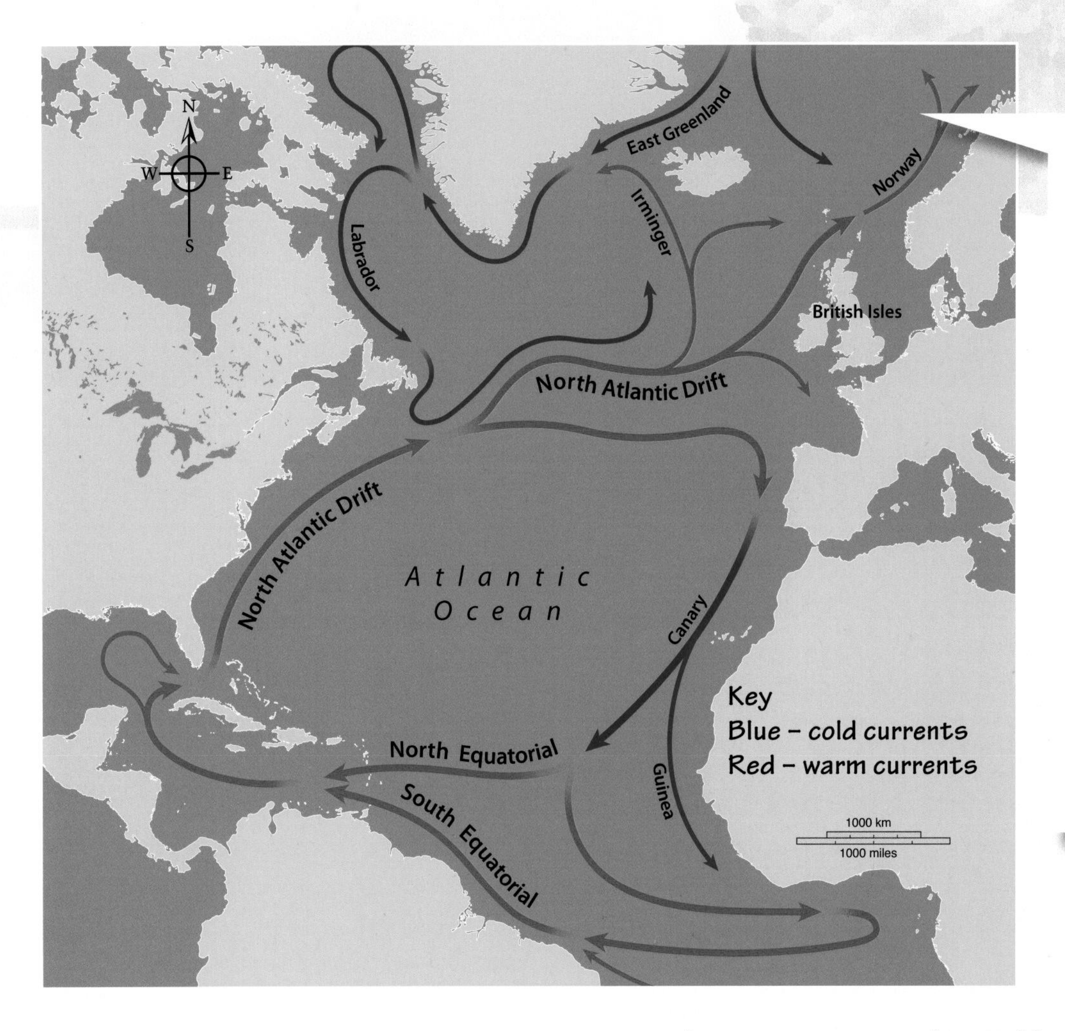

The North Atlantic Drift is a warm current that flows north-eastwards from the Mexican coast and across the Atlantic Ocean, warming the coasts of western Europe. This map shows the direction of the warm currents. Without the North Atlantic Drift, Britain and Ireland would be several degrees colder than they are today.

Temperatures on the coast are also affected by ocean currents flowing offshore. These currents are warm or cold water flowing through the oceans. Warm currents flow from tropical oceans. Cold currents flow from polar regions.

Wildlife on coasts

Rockpools are like miniature sea worlds. Plants and animals have to adapt to changing conditions as tides rise and fall.

Rocky and sandy shorelines are home to hundreds of different creatures. Off the shore, tiny plants and animals called **plankton** float just below the surface. These small creatures provide food for many larger animals, from fish to the great whales.

Rocky coasts are particularly rich in wildlife. Seaweeds, shrimps, starfish and anemones live in rockpools on the shore. Seals climb onto rocks to bask in the sunshine. Seabirds nest on narrow ledges on steep cliffs.

Worms, crabs and shellfish hide in the sand on beaches, or in the mud of **estuaries**. These small creatures provide food for birds such as gulls, that can open shells with their sharp beaks. Tough plants, such as marram grass, root among the dunes behind the beach.

JACQUES COUSTEAU

Jacques Cousteau (1910-1997) was a French diver and film-maker. He made films and TV programmes about undersea wildlife. He also helped to invent the aqualung, which divers use to breathe underwater.

*Birds nest on cliffs in large, noisy groups called **colonies**. These albatrosses are nesting on the Falklands Islands, where there is plenty of food to feed their chicks.*

Using the coast

People use coasts in many different ways. The sea provides food such as fish, shellfish and seaweed. Salt, which we use to flavour food, also comes from the sea.

Fishermen haul in their catch off the coast of Canada.

Metals, such as copper, tin and nickel are mined from the seabed. Gold and even diamonds are found on some coasts. Oil and natural gas are found in rocks under the seabed. Oil rigs drill into the rocks to reach the oil or gas, which is then pumped to the surface.

PEARL DIVERS

Pearls are natural gems made by shellfish called oysters. The pearl grows around a piece of grit inside the oyster's shell. Throughout history people have dived down to collect pearls from the sea bed. Today, the oysters are often reared on special 'farms'.

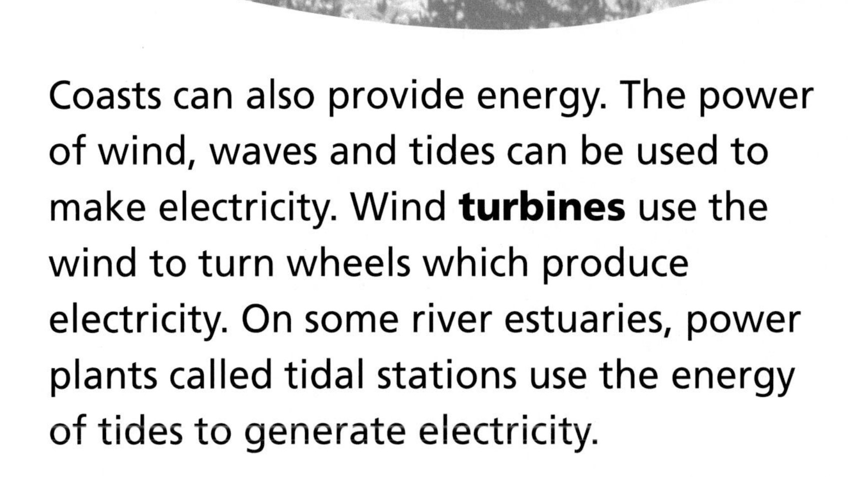

This power station on the coast of La Rance, France, uses the energy of crashing waves to produce electricity.

Coasts can also provide energy. The power of wind, waves and tides can be used to make electricity. Wind **turbines** use the wind to turn wheels which produce electricity. On some river estuaries, power plants called tidal stations use the energy of tides to generate electricity.

Living on coasts

People have lived on coasts for thousands of years. As well as food, coasts provide transport. For centuries, the sea has been used as a watery highway. Towns and villages grew up on sheltered harbours and along rivers, which could be used to transport people and goods inland.

UNBELIEVABLE!

One-fifth of all the people in the world live on the coast. In some countries the number is even higher. A third of all the people in Britain live within a few kilometres of the coast. The Ganges Delta Bangladesh is barely above sea level and about one-third of the country floods in the rainy season.

Many of the world's largest cities, such as Sydney, Australia, have grown up on the coast.

Over time, villages and towns grew into busy ports, with docks stretching along the coast or a river. Factories sprang up to use goods that arrived by water. Many coastal cities are now very crowded, with high-rise buildings lining the shore.

Cranes are used to load and unload cargo from ships at busy ports.

Tourism is an important industry on many coasts. In the 1950s, cheap air travel began, and people started going abroad for their holidays. **Resorts** grew up on beautiful beaches the world over. In the 1950s, Benidorm on the Spanish coast was a small, peaceful fishing village. Now it is a huge tourist resort.

Dangerous coasts

Coasts can be dangerous places to live! High tides and storms bring risks from flooding. In warm parts of the world, huge whirling storms called **hurricanes** may sweep in off the ocean. The spinning air sucks up a mound of water below it. This acts like a high tide when the storm hits the coast.

The Maldives are a group of islands in the Indian Ocean. In the future, rising sea levels could threaten small islands such as this one.

This map shows how the coast of Florida, in southeastern USA, would change if sea levels rose by 6 metres. Many towns would be underwater.

A tsunami, caused by the Indian Ocean earthquake in 2004, wrecked this town on the coast of Indonesia, in southeast Asia.

The risk of coastal flooding is now growing because sea levels are rising. Scientists believe warmer weather is to blame. Gases from factories, cars and power stations have built up in the air and are trapping more of the Sun's heat. This is causing the world to get warmer. Ice in the polar regions has begun to melt, which is adding more water to the oceans.

Undersea earthquakes and volcanoes can produce giant waves called **tsunamis**. These huge waves sweep across the ocean to batter towns on distant coasts.

UNBELIEVABLE!

In 2004, an earthquake shook the bed of the Indian Ocean. A tsunami spread right across the ocean to wreck coastal towns thousands of kilometres away. More than 200,000 people died in this terrible disaster.

Taking care of coasts

People can damage both coasts and their wildlife. For centuries, people have dumped rubbish in coastal seas. Towns, farms and factories also empty waste into rivers that ends up in the sea. People drop litter on the beach. This problem is called **pollution**.

The Great Barrier Reef protects 350 different kinds of coral and more than 1,000 species of fish.

UNBELIEVABLE!

Accidents at sea can cause a lot of pollution. In 1996, an oil tanker called the Sea Empress was wrecked off the coast of Wales. Over 70,000 tonnes of oil spilled into the sea and washed up on the Pembrokeshire coast. Thousands of seals and seabirds died.

Waste and litter can harm plants and animals. Most people now realise that coasts need our protection. Many countries follow rules that control the amount of waste that reaches the sea. This is helping wildlife on coasts.

Nature reserves and parks have been set up to protect beautiful coastlines. In the 1970s, the Great Barrier Reef off the coast of Australia became a huge nature reserve. In Britain, the Pembrokeshire National Park protects 600 square kilometres of coastline in Wales.

Beaches are now checked for pollution. The blue flag shows that this beach is clean and safe for swimming.

Explore life at the seaside!

Using a map

Look at this map of a coastline. What does it tell you about the scenery? Look for headlands, bays, beaches and islands. Can you tell if the coast is rocky or sandy? Can you see estuaries, where rivers meet the sea? Is the coast wild and undeveloped, or can you see ports, towns or resorts?

Look at the location of towns and villages. Why do you think they have grown up in these places? Does the map show things to do when you visit the coast?

This stretch of coastline in Wales is a national park. It has beautiful scenery, including rocky headlands, estuaries, bays and islands, which you can see on this map.

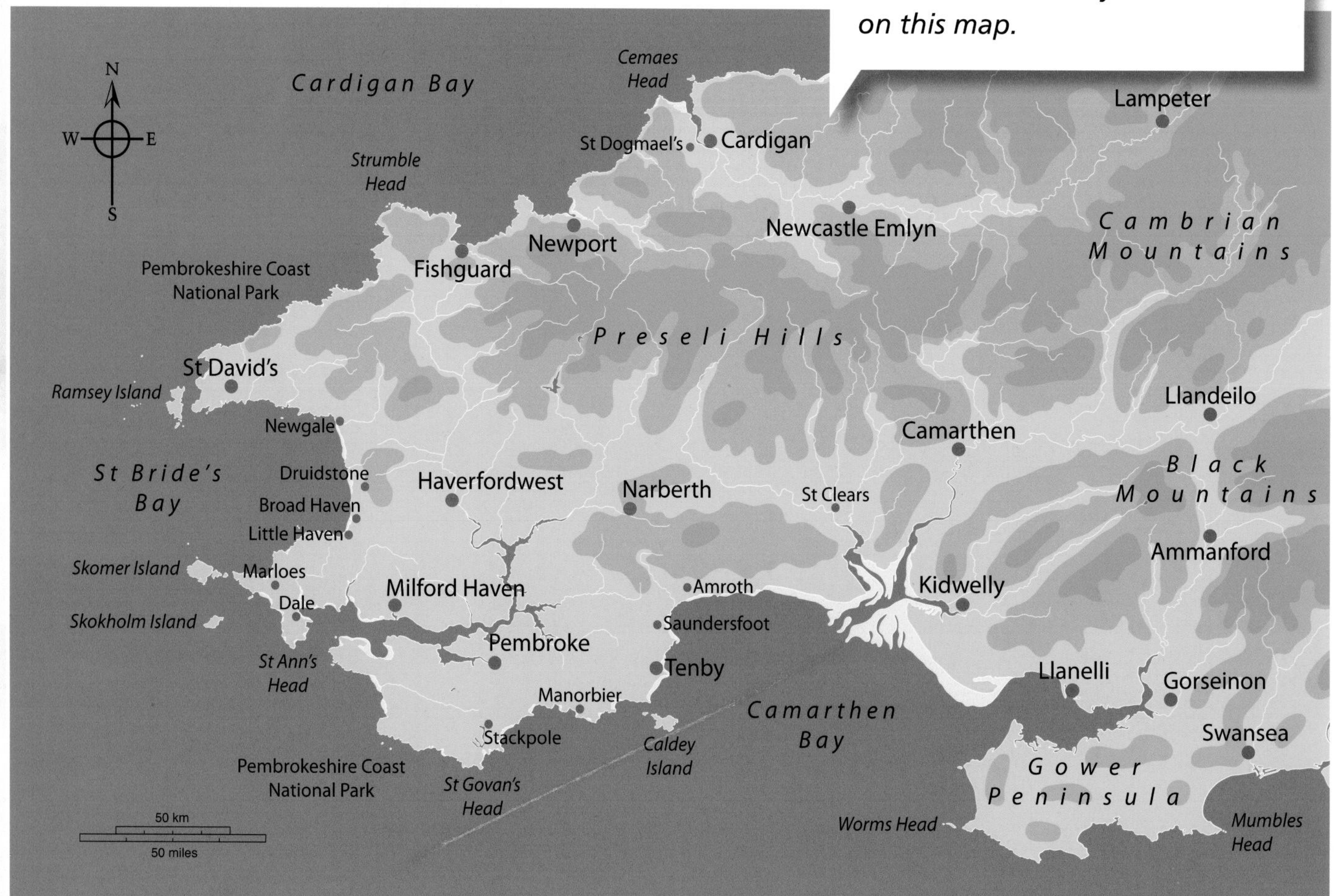

Fish, shrimps, snails, sea anemones and seaweed all live in rockpools. What can you find?

Go to the seaside

Find out about wildlife on the coast on your next trip to the seaside. Different plants and animals live by the water, at the high tide mark, and on cliffs and sand dunes behind the beach.

Is the beach pebbly or sandy? Worms and shells hide in the sand or mud, but you can see the holes they leave at the surface. Look for the tracks of birds and other animals. See how many creatures you can find living in a rockpool.

Warning
Always beware of the tide while looking at life on the beach.

Cross-curricular links

Use this topic web to investigate coasts in other parts of your curriculum.

Citizenship
Find out more about how litter can harm coasts and wildlife. Then make a poster explaining why people should not drop litter.

English & ICT
Find out more about a particular hurricane or tsunami using your local library or the Internet. Write about the event as if you had been there.

Art
Draw a picture of coastal scenery in the style of a famous artist such as Claude Monet or Georges Seurat.

COASTS

History
Use the Internet or books at the library to find out about a city on the coast. What work do people do there, and how has this work changed over the years?

Design & Technology
Draw a map of your favourite beach or coast in the middle of a large piece of paper. Draw pictures or take photos of coastal scenery, plants and animals, and stick them around the map.

Science
Use a library or the Internet to find out more about why sea levels are rising. What can be done to protect coasts from erosion and the sea?

Glossary

Bay A place where the coast curves inward.

Cliff A steep rock face.

Coastal About coasts.

Colony A large group of animals living close together.

Cove A small bay.

Debris Small bits of broken material, such as pebbles.

Delta A flat area of land at a river mouth, made of silt.

Deposition When a river drops its silt to form a delta.

Dune A mound of wind-blown sand, found at the back of a beach.

Dyke A bank built to prevent flooding or keep back the sea.

Erosion When the land is worn away by wind, water or ice.

Erupt When lava and ash shoot out from an active volcano.

Estuary The mouth or lower part of a river, washed by the tide.

Gravity The natural pull of the Earth, Moon or Sun, which tugs on other objects, such as the sea.

Groyne A wooden fence on a beach which helps to prevent erosion.

Headland Part of the coast which sticks out into the sea.

Hurricane A revolving tropical storm.

Lava Hot, melted rock erupted by volcanoes.

Longshore drift The sideways movement of sand or pebbles along the coast, due to waves striking the shore at an angle.

Marina A harbour built to shelter yachts and other boats.

Mudflat A muddy bank, often found near the mouth of a river.

Plankton Tiny plants and animals that float under the surface of the sea.

Pollution When something harms the air, water or soil.

Resort A holiday town or village, often on the coast.

Sea level The height of the sea along a coastline.

Silt Very small, rocky debris such as mud.

Stack A pillar of rock in the sea.

Temperature How cold or hot it is.

Tide The rise and fall of the sea on the coast.

Tsunami A giant wave caused by an undersea earthquake or erupting volcano.

Turbine A machine for making electricity that can be driven by wind, water or steam.

Index

Further information

Books

Nature Trail: Seaside by Jen Green, Wayland, 2010

Look around you: Seaside by Ruth Thomson, Wayland, 2007

Geography Detective Investigates: Coastlines by Jen Green, Wayland, 2007

Geography First: Coasts by Nicola Edwards, Wayland, 2006

Websites

Enchanted Learning website has facts about coasts, oceans, tsunamis and hurricanes:

http://www.enchantedlearning.com/

National Trust webpage on coasts has information about wildlife, walks and much more:

http://www.nationaltrust.org.uk/main/w-chl/w-countryside_environment/w-coastline.htm